745.4
0003684

artfile

Patterns

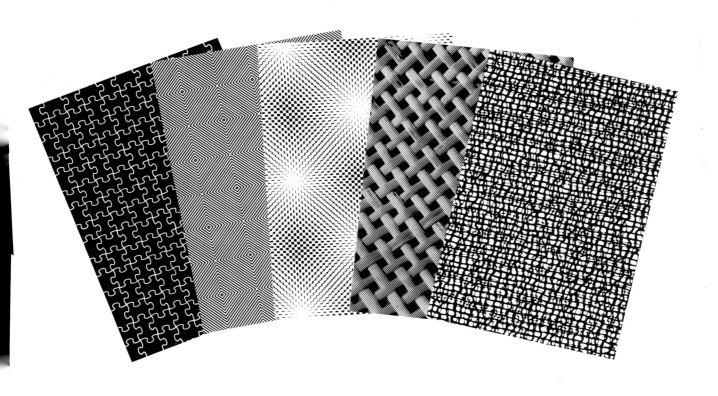

*Ready-to-use,
copyright-free art & graphics
for the busy, budget-wise
designer.*

Φ

PHAIDON • OXFORD

Published by
Phaidon Press Limited
Musterlin House
Jordan Hill Road
Oxford
England
OX2 8DP

First published 1990

© **Graphic Books International Ltd.**
P.O. Box 349
Newlands Building
Lowlands
Guernsey
Channel Islands (UK)

A CIP catalogue record for this
book is available from the
British Library

ISBN 0 7148 2670 7

Printed in Great Britain by
Penshurst Press Ltd.
Tunbridge Wells, Kent

The art of using

artfile

This book is just one in a series of Artfiles, each of which provides hundreds of ready-to-use images designed to add an instant professional touch to print, publicity and all forms of graphic communication at a fraction of the cost of original art.

All of the images contained in this book are yours to use in almost any way you wish. No reproduction fees are required and the copyright will not be infringed, provided that the Artfile images are not incorporated into any form of product or service that could be considered by the publishers or copyright-holder as an alternative or competitive art source.

When using Artfile images as part of a design service for fee-paying clients, it is advisable that clients are made fully aware that the designs in part or whole are not unique, exclusive or their copyright.

Creating original illustrations and graphics has always been time consuming and expensive, but with Artfile you have hundreds of images at your fingertips for less than the cost of one single piece of original art.

With Artfile, even the inexperienced non-designer can quickly and easily transform newsletters, advertisements, leaflets, etc. into effective commnications. Experienced designers will appreciate the numerous ways in which each illustration can be reproduced and modified but for those who have limited creative skills and knowledge of reproduction techniques, we offer the following advice.

Firstly, take time to familiarise yourself with the contents of each book. This will help you to create ideas that spring from material that you have available rather than trying to find images to meet pre- conceived ideas. The miniature visual index provided with each volume will help you to find illustrations in just a few seconds. If you purchase several Artfile volumes, we would suggest either that copies are made of the index pages or that they are removed to create a master index.

How you use your Artfile art will depend on your personal working methods. The majority of users may wish to separate the art sheets and place them in a ring binder or filing system. Breaking down the book into individual

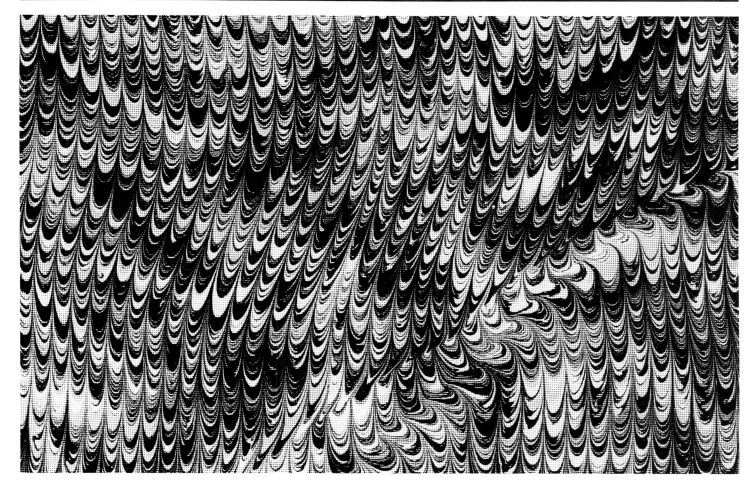

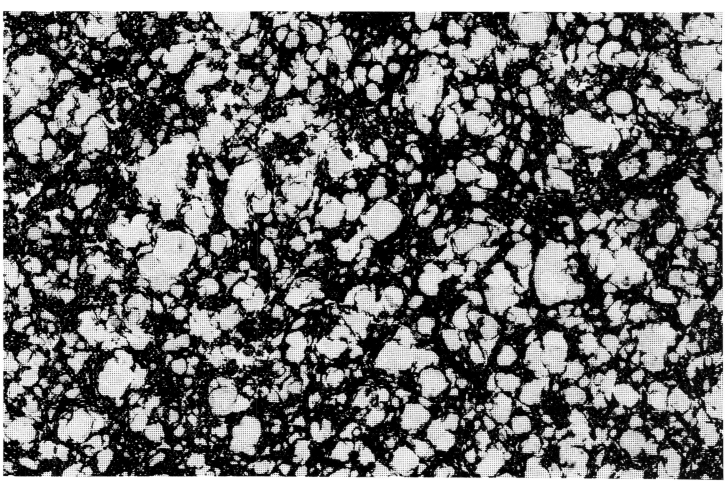

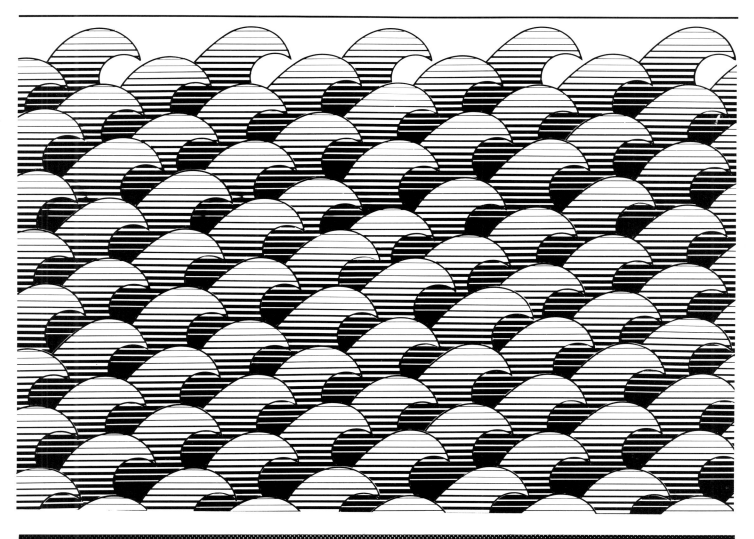

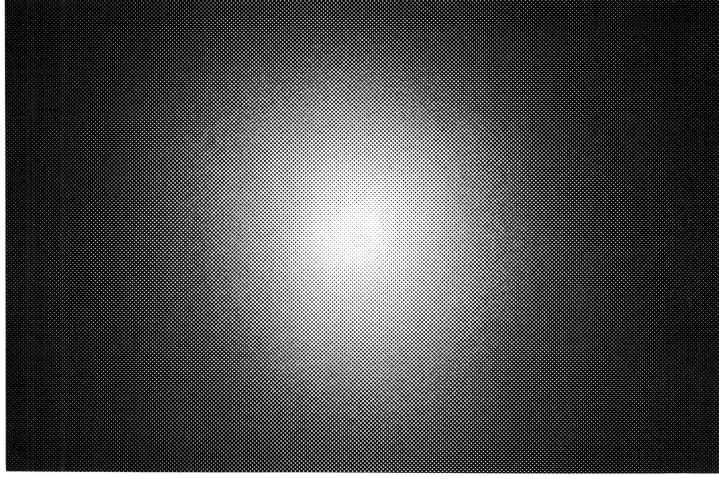

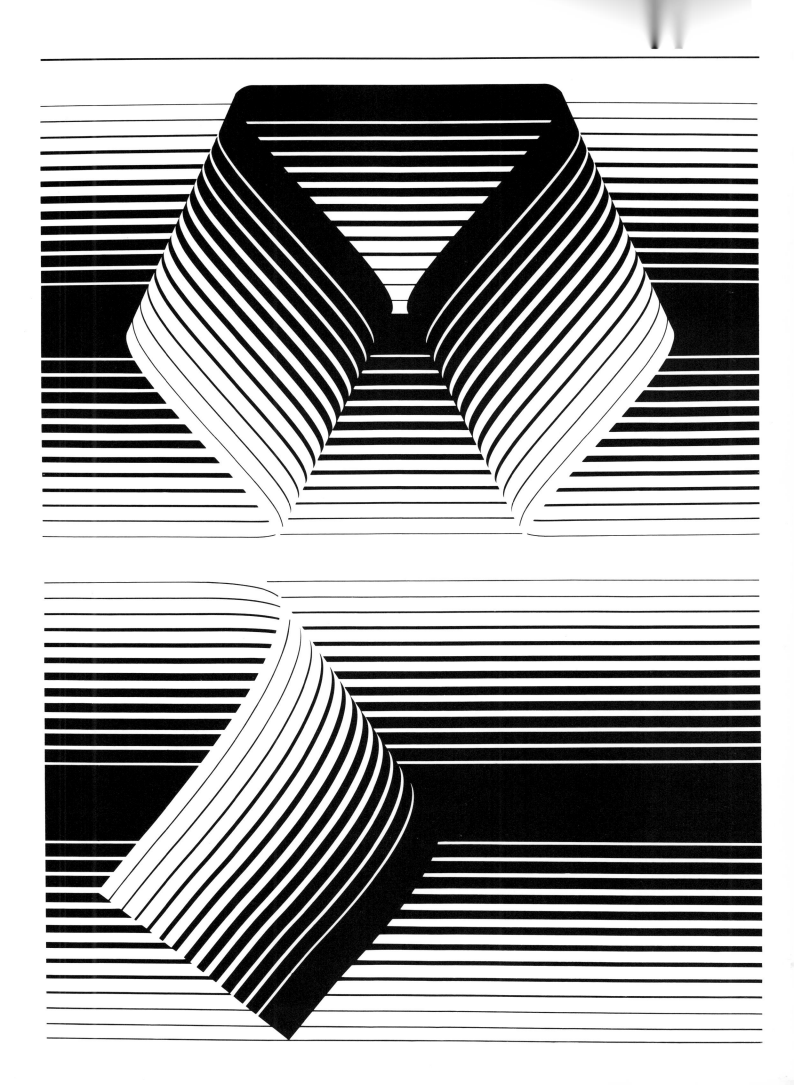

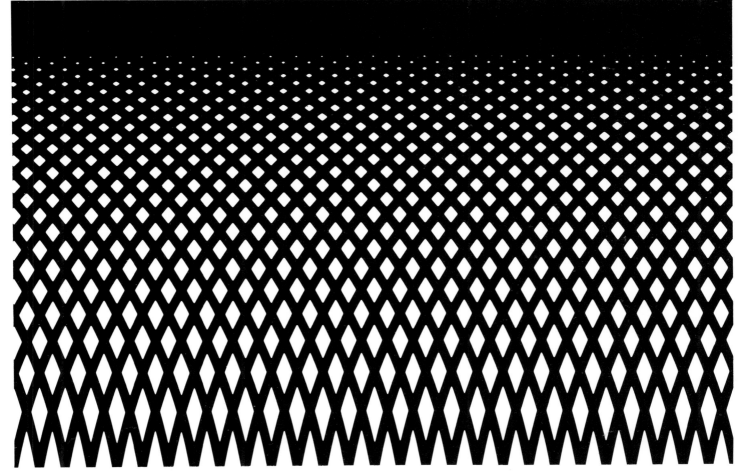

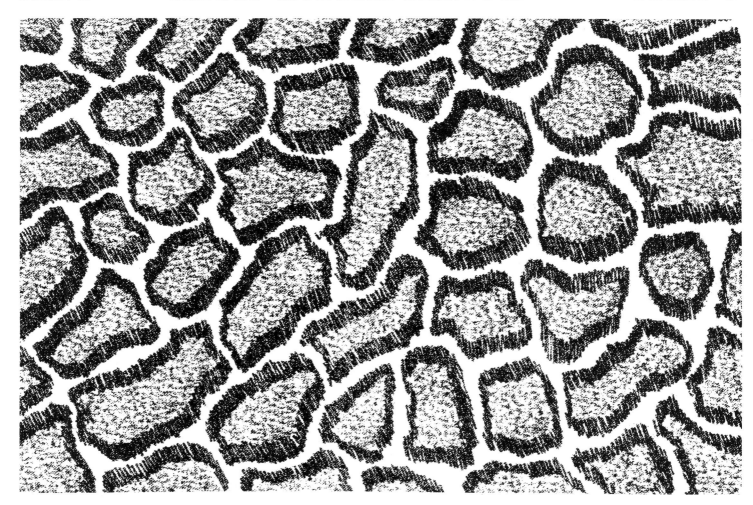

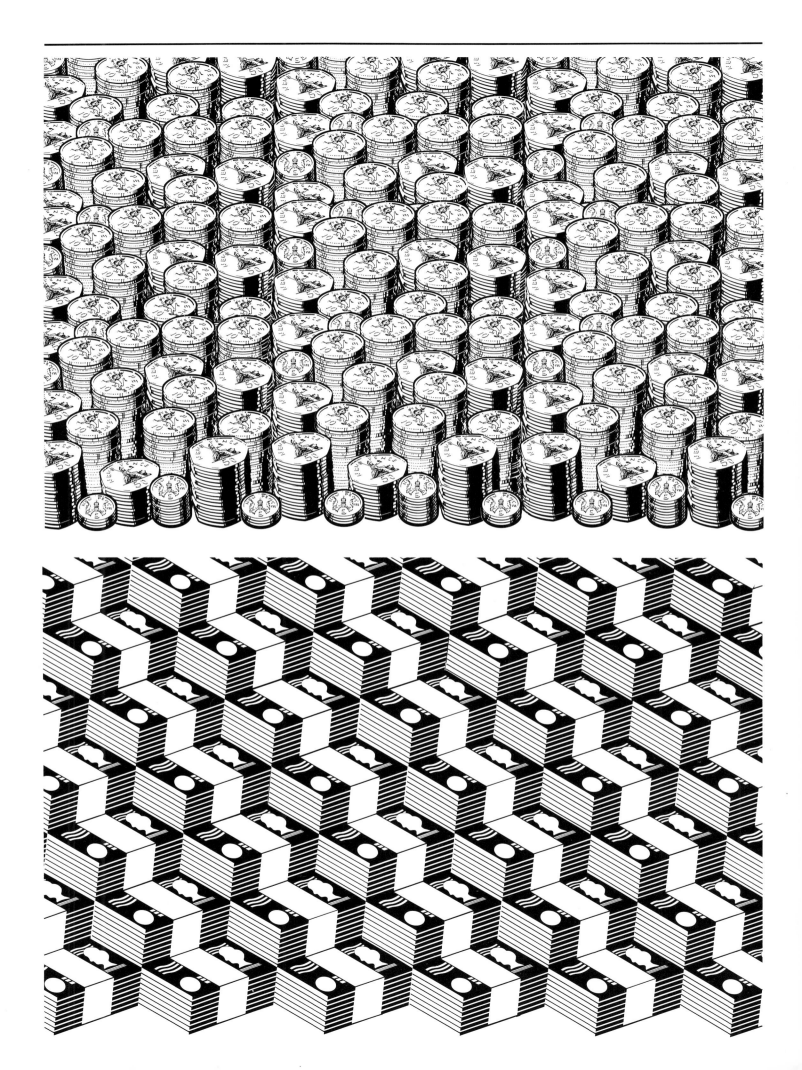

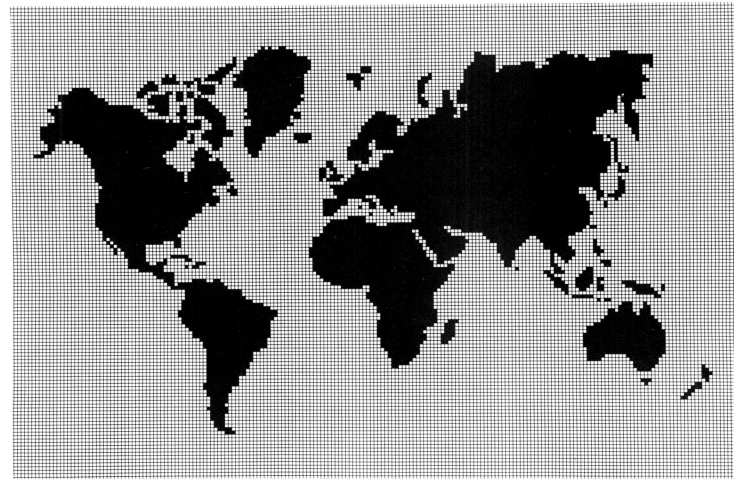

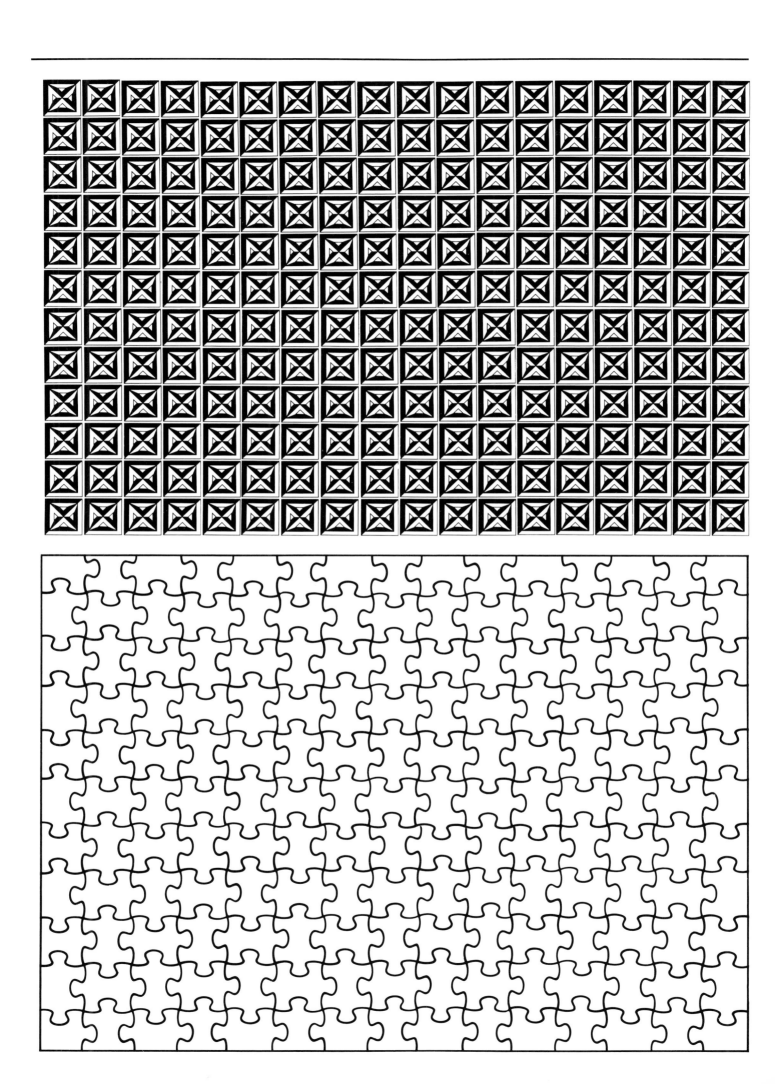

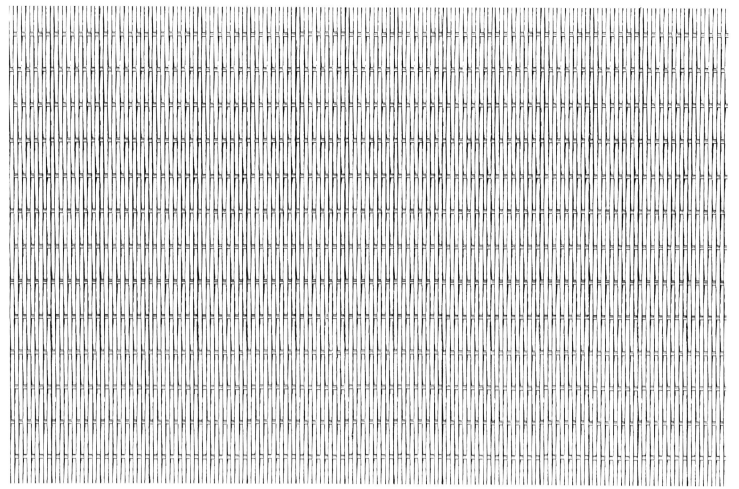

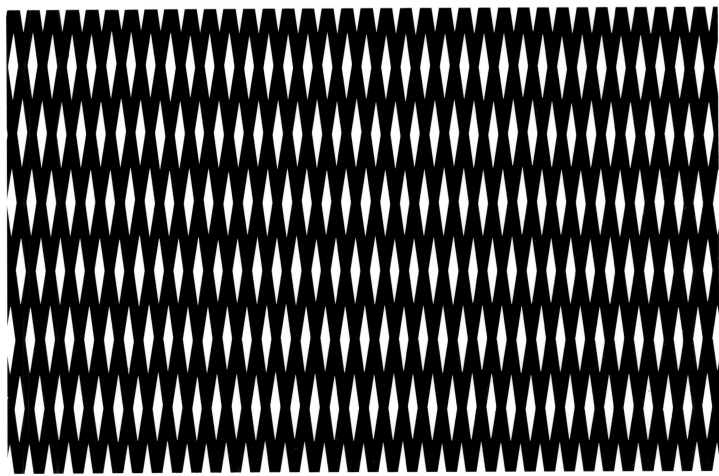

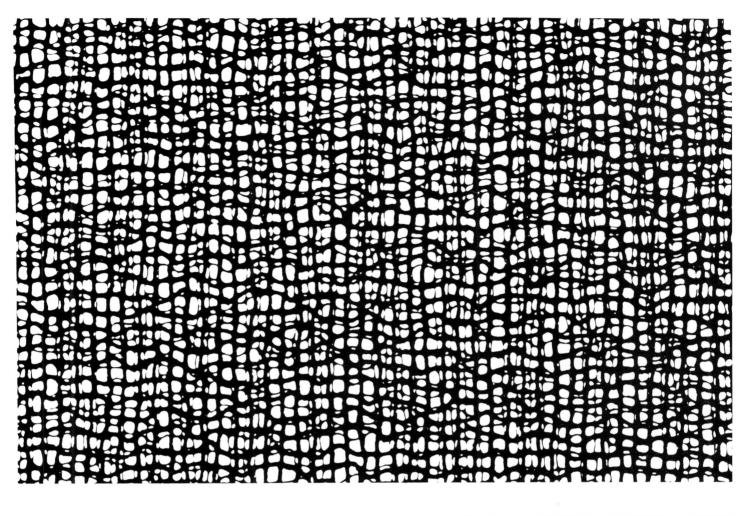

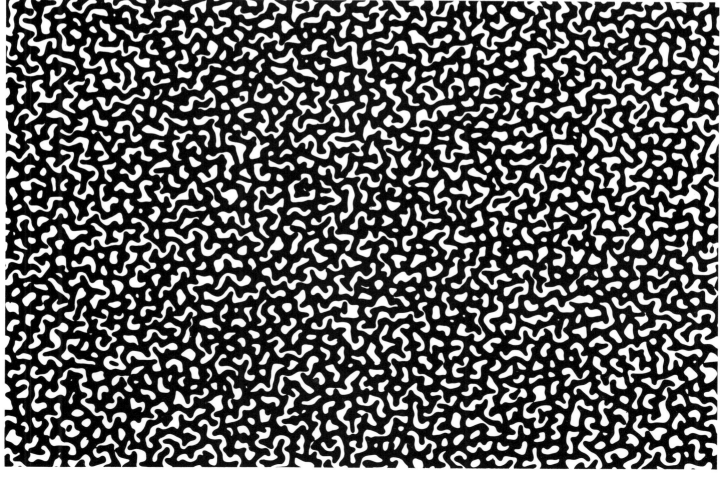

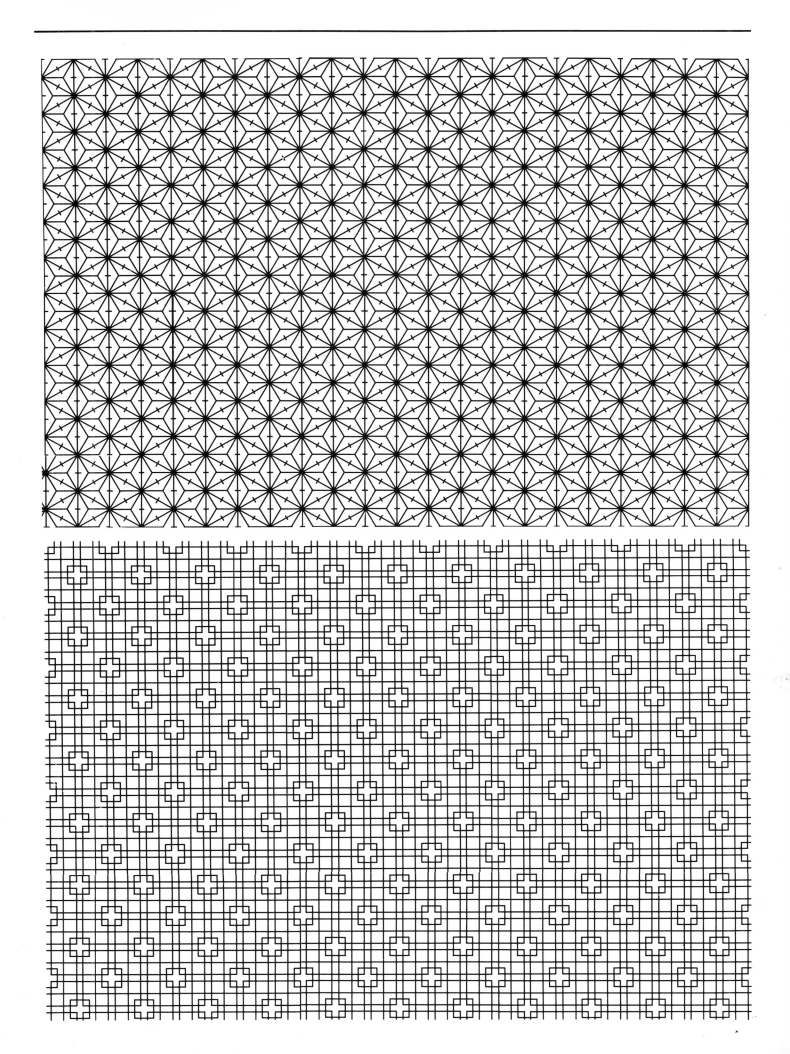

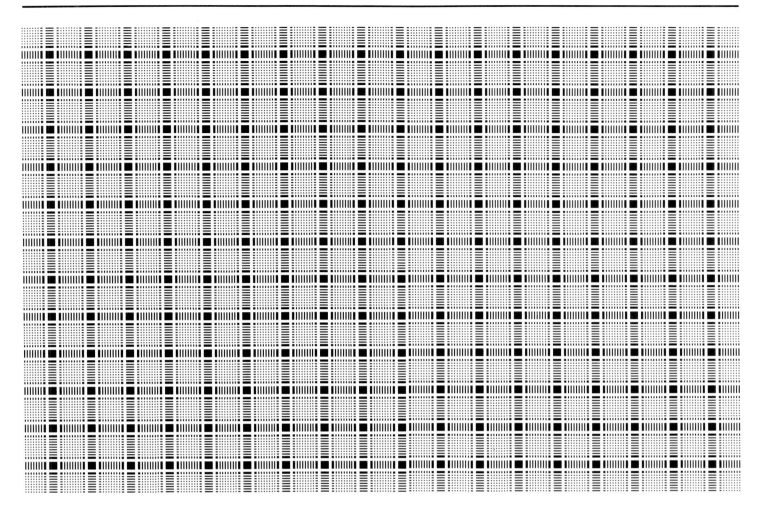

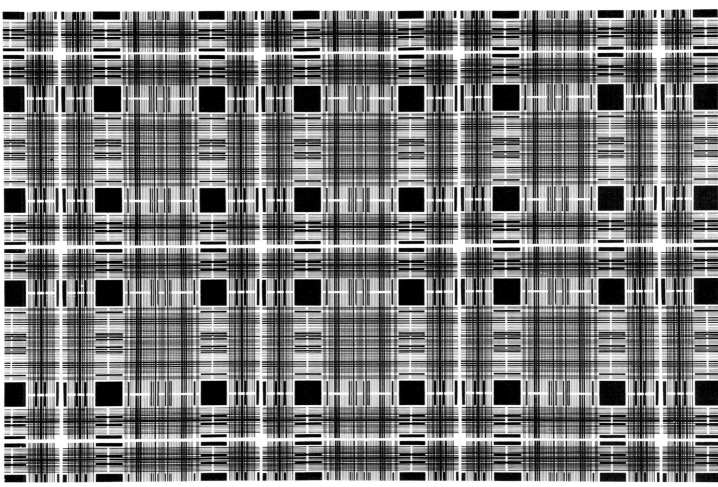

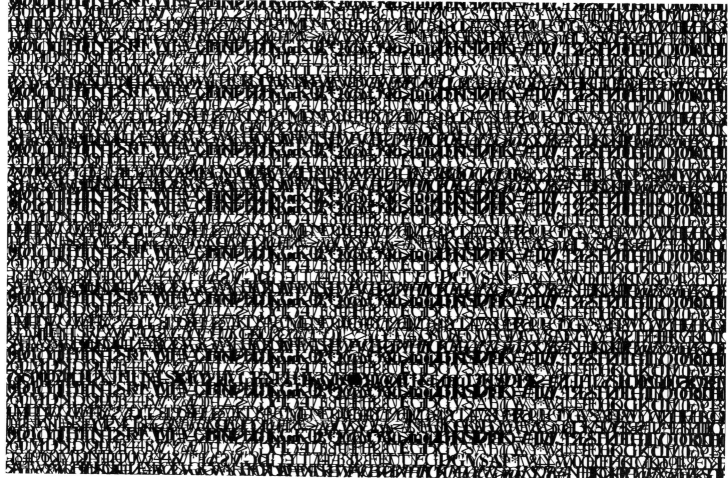

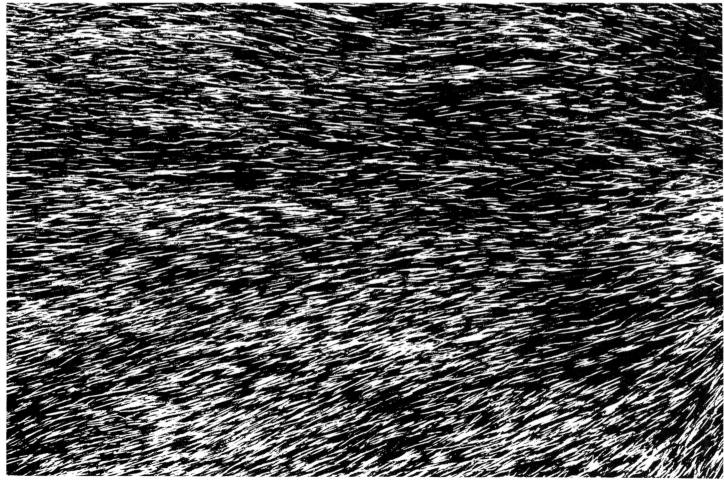

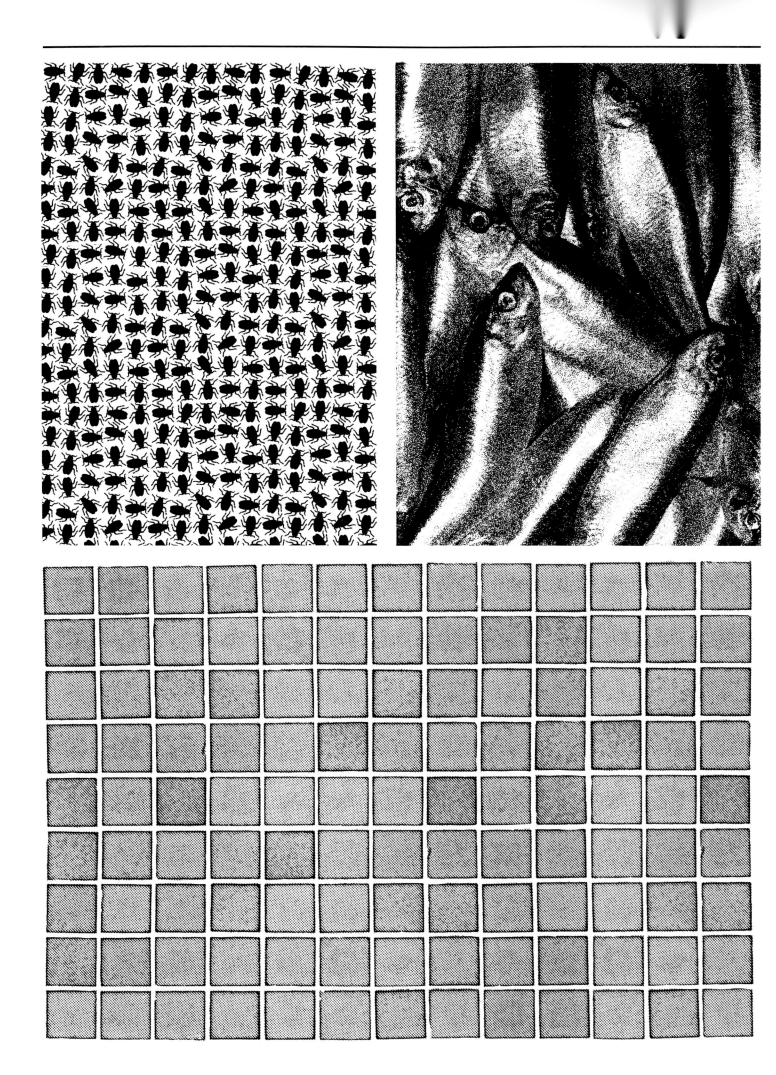

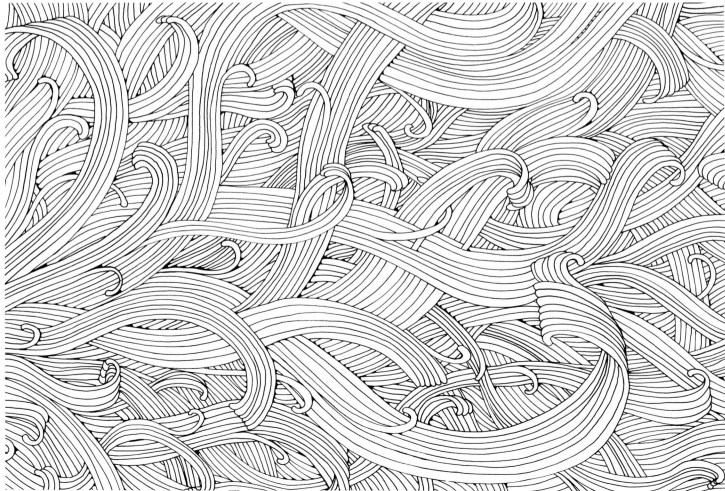

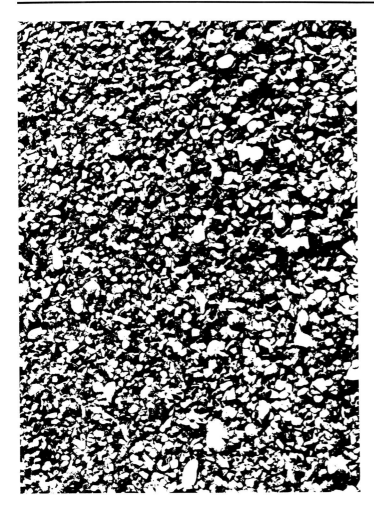

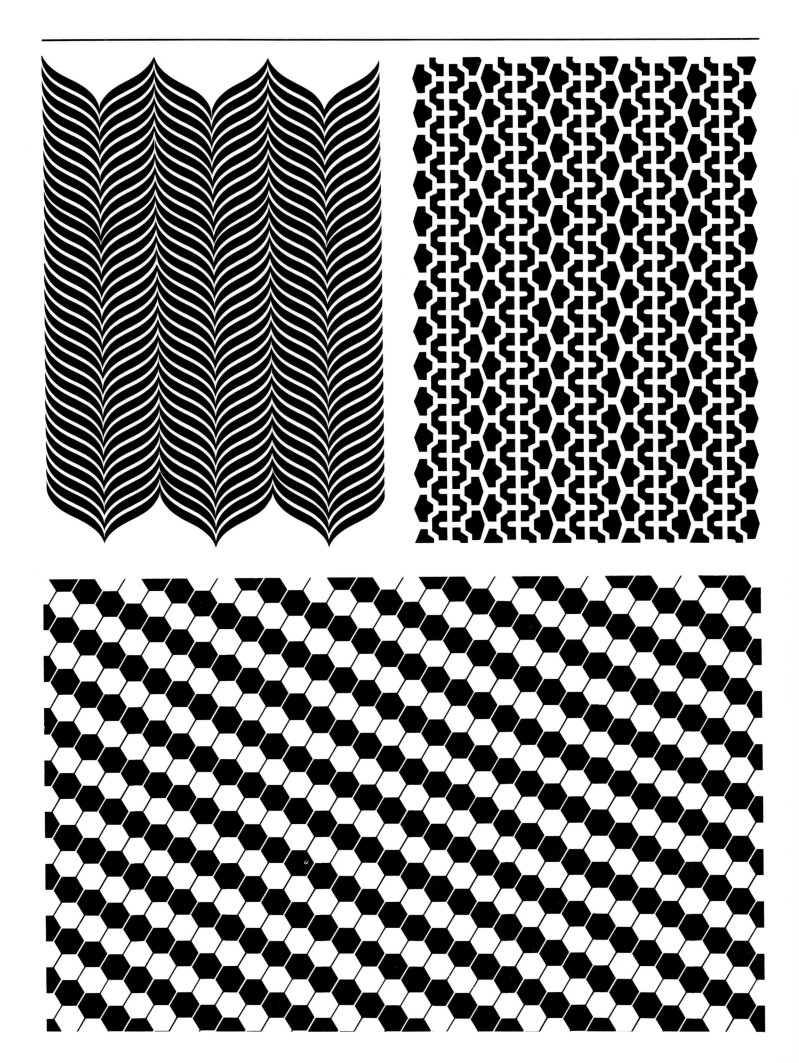

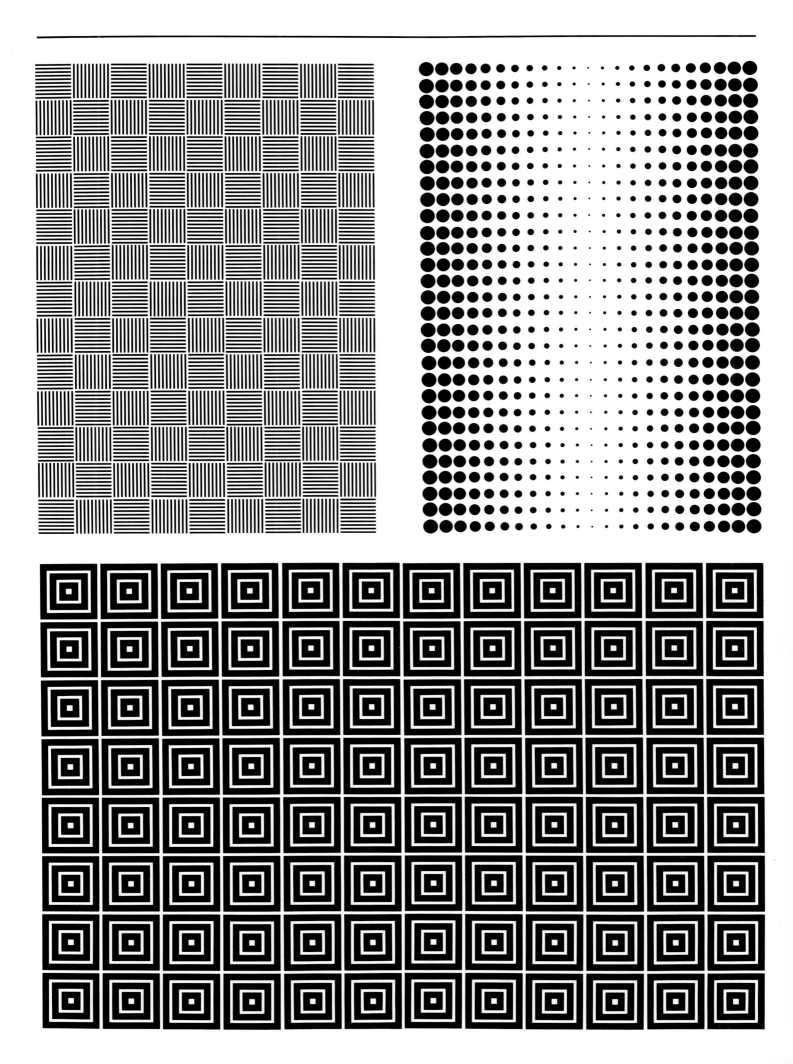

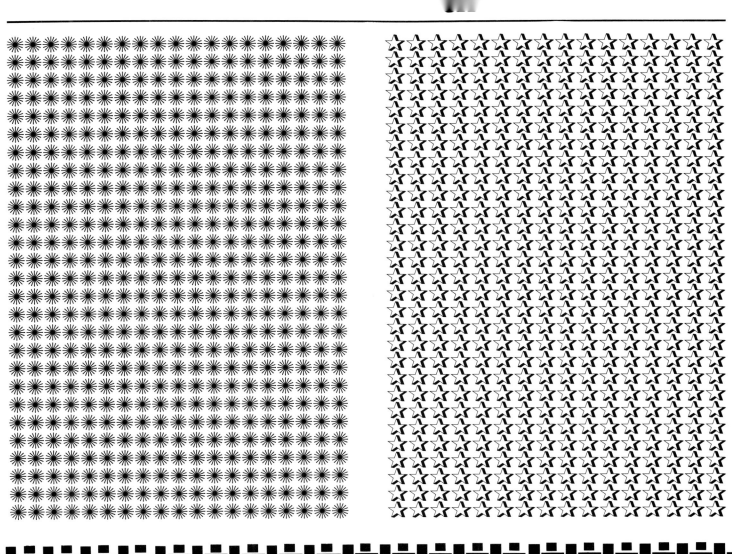

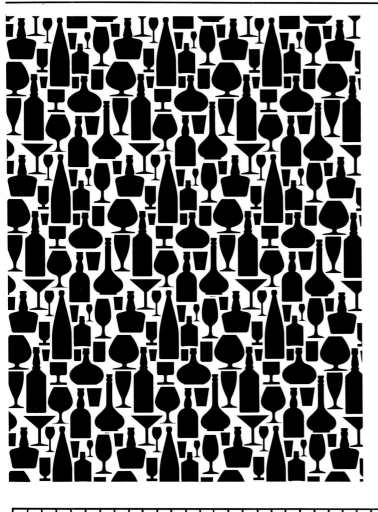
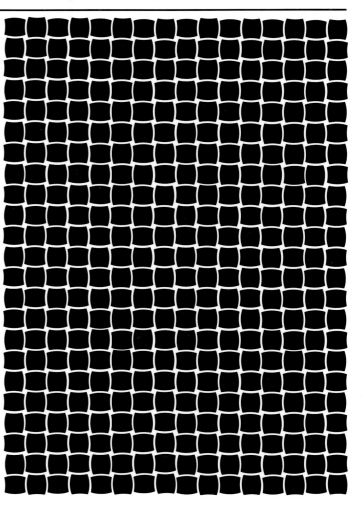
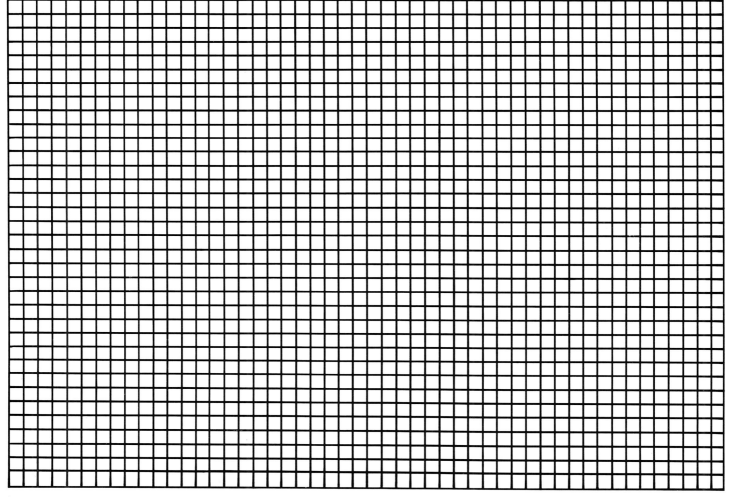

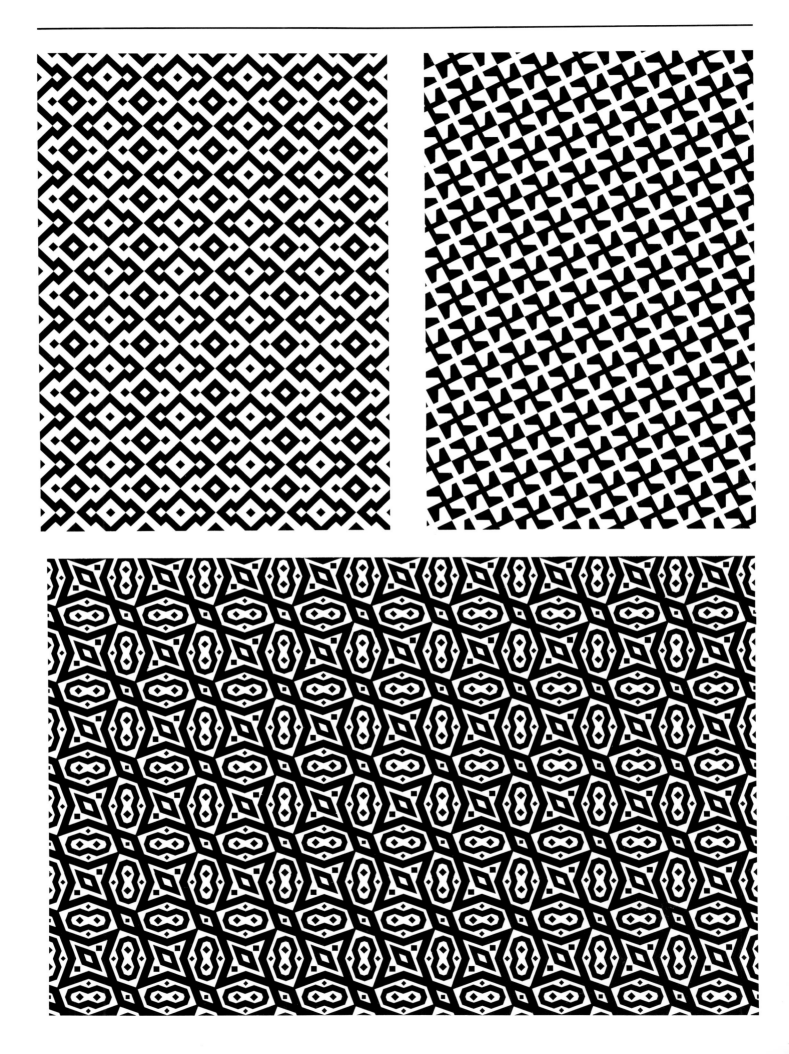

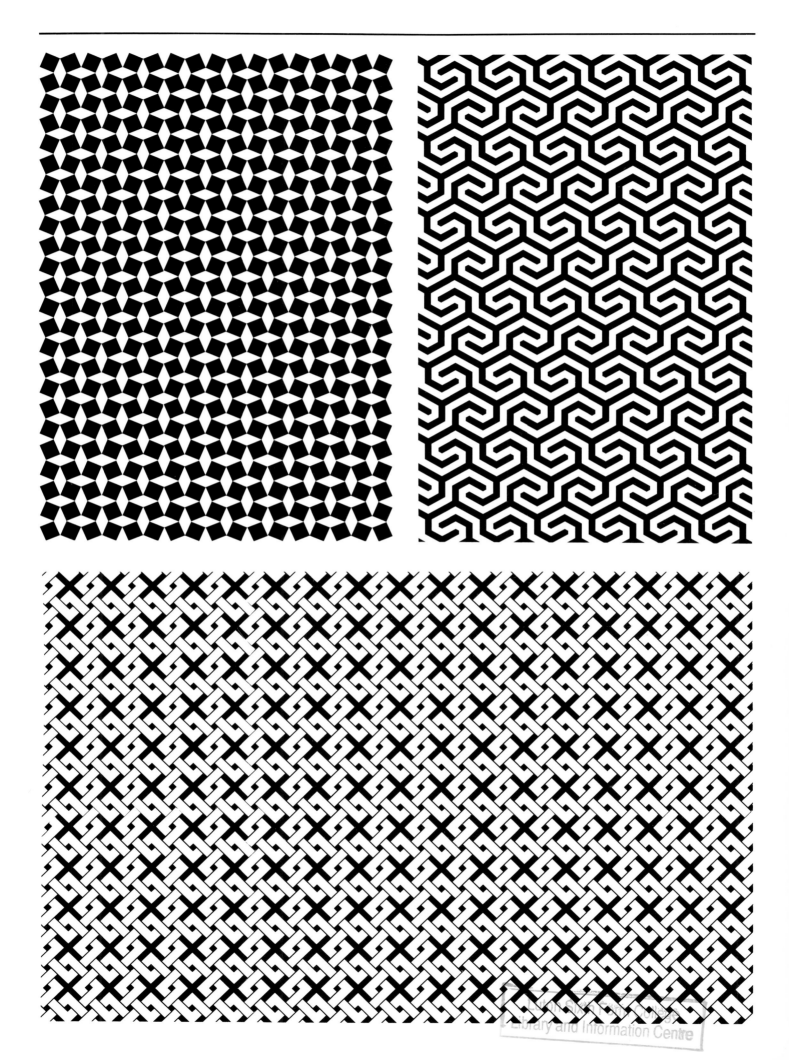

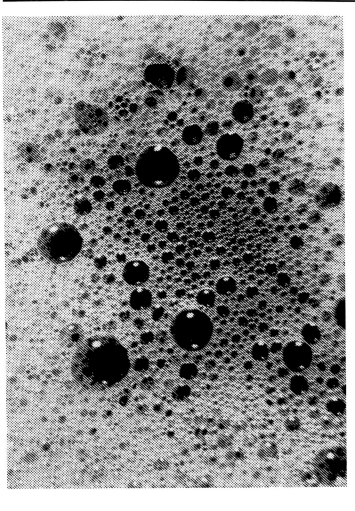
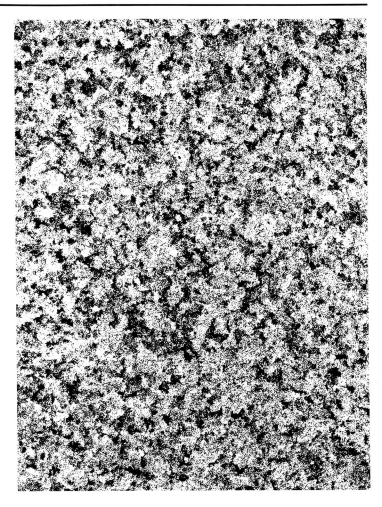

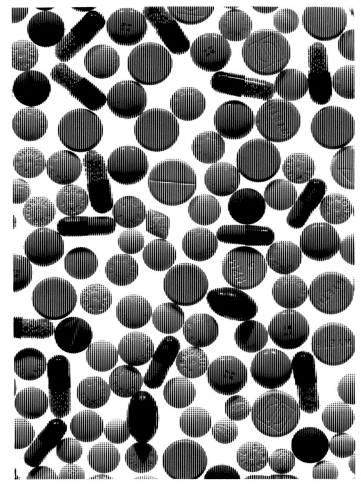

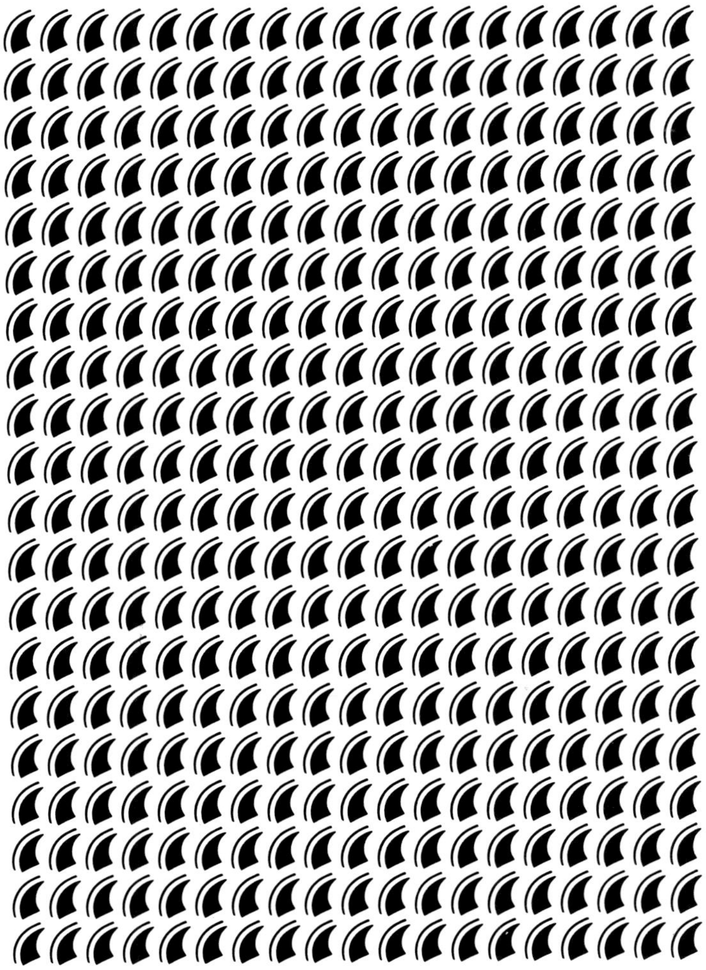
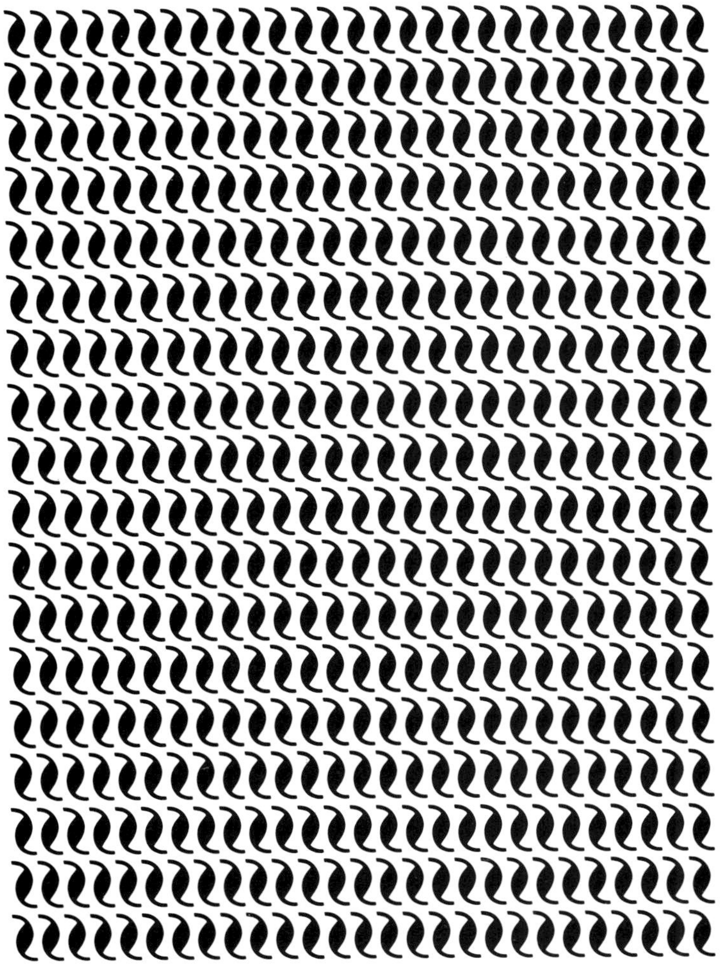
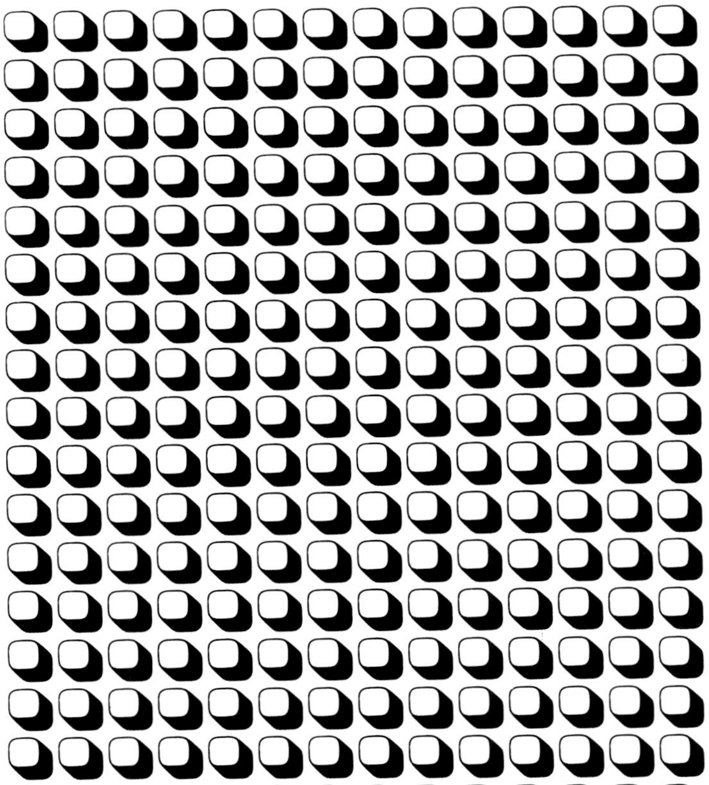
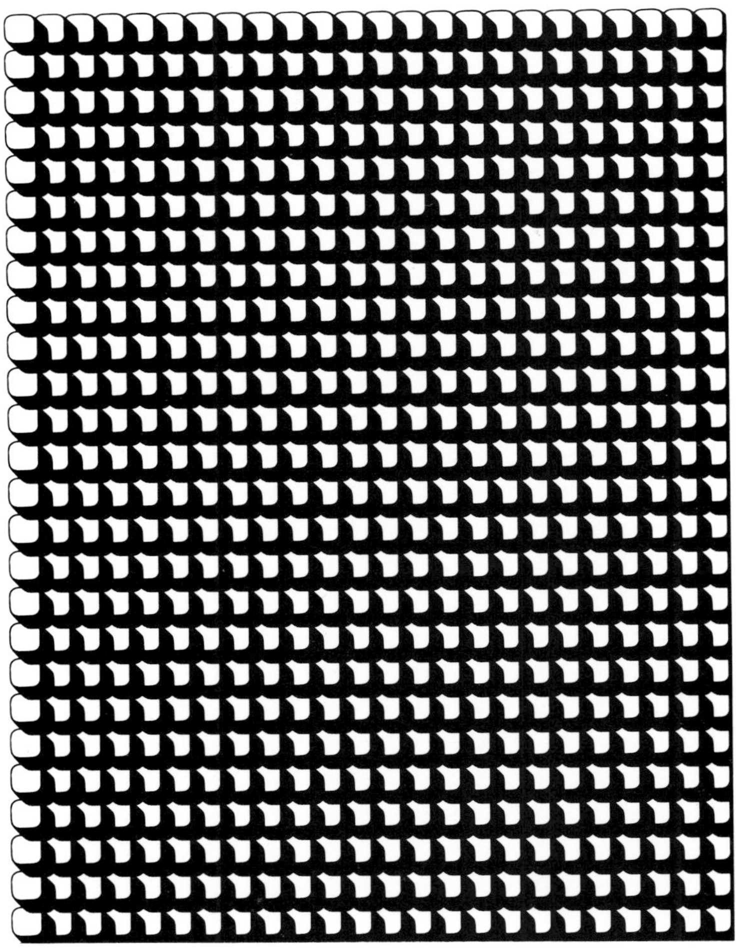

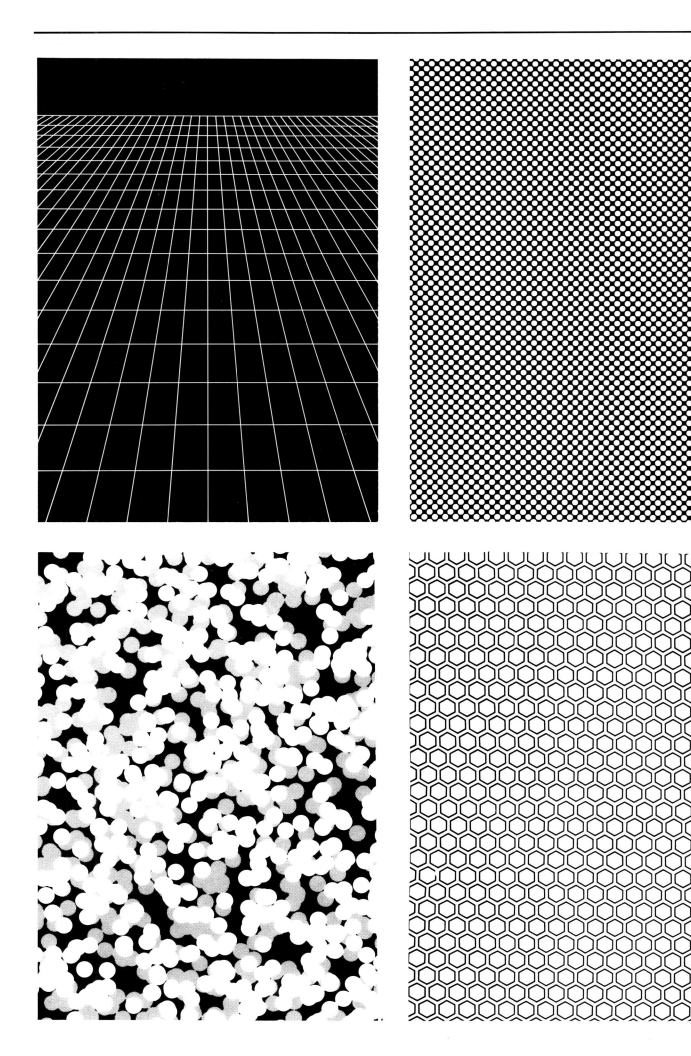

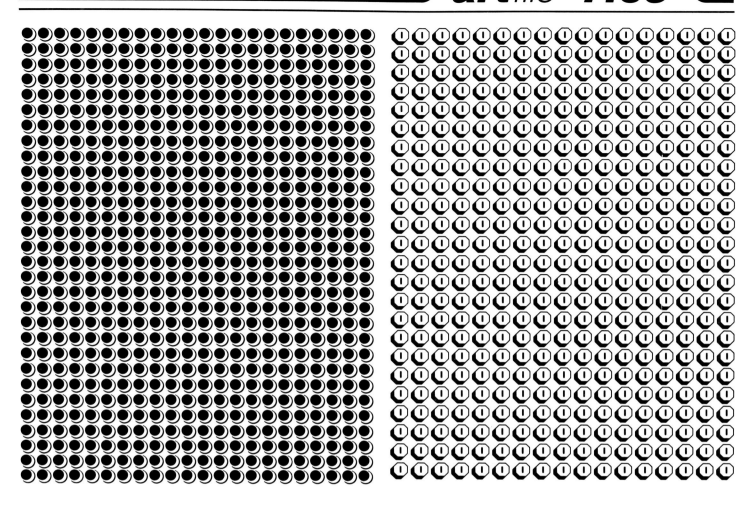

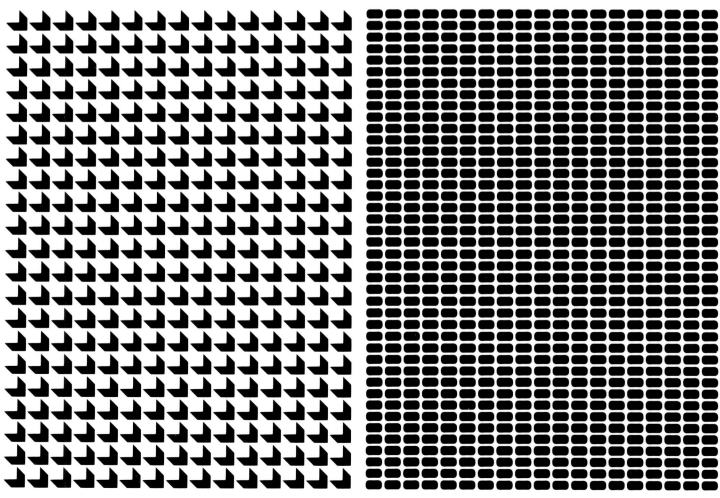

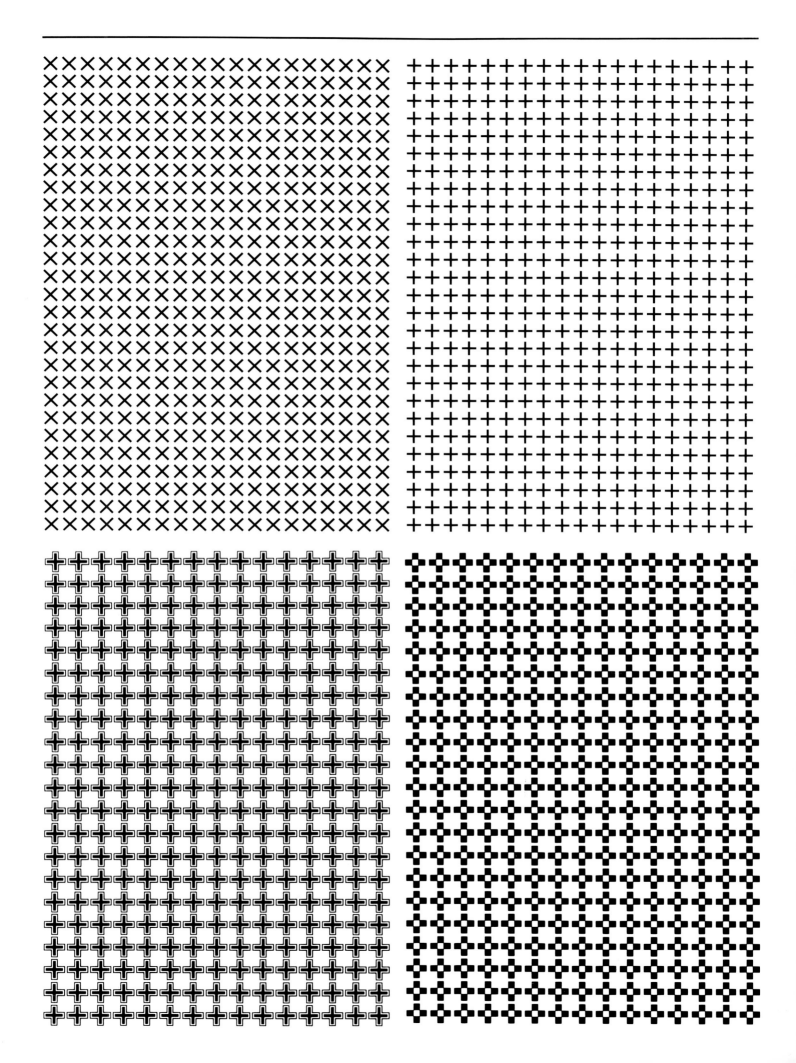

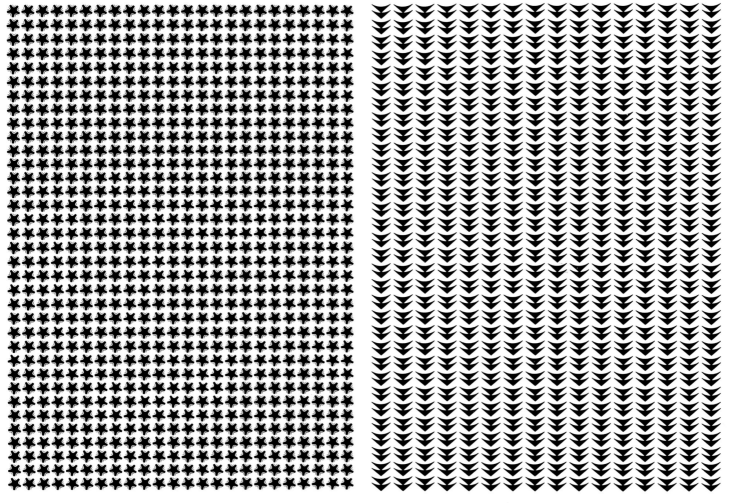

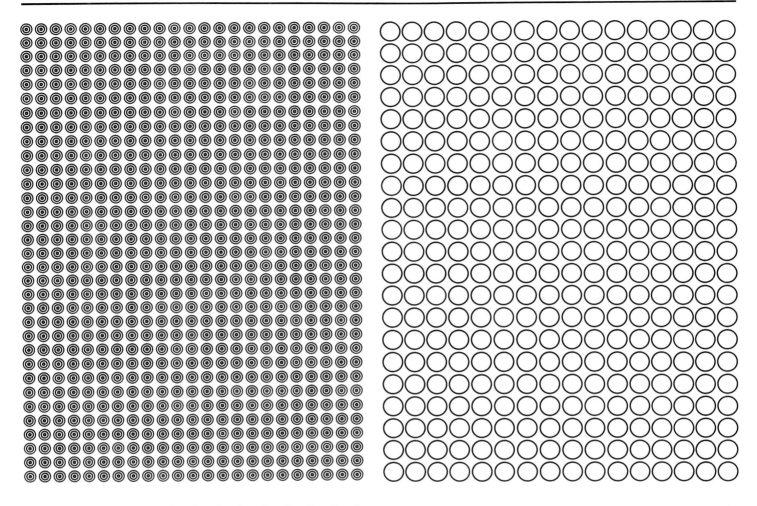

SPECIMENSPECIMENSPECIMENSPECIMEN
IMENSPECIMENSPECIMENSPECIMENSPEC
SPECIMENSPECIMENSPECIMENSPECIMEN
IMENSPECIMENSPECIMENSPECIMENSPEC
SPECIMENSPECIMENSPECIMENSPECIMEN
IMENSPECIMENSPECIMENSPECIMENSPEC
SPECIMENSPECIMENSPECIMENSPECIMEN
IMENSPECIMENSPECIMENSPECIMENSPEC
SPECIMENSPECIMENSPECIMENSPECIMEN
IMENSPECIMENSPECIMENSPECIMENSPEC
SPECIMENSPECIMENSPECIMENSPECIMEN
IMENSPECIMENSPECIMENSPECIMENSPEC
SPECIMENSPECIMENSPECIMENSPECIMEN
IMENSPECIMENSPECIMENSPECIMENSPEC
SPECIMENSPECIMENSPECIMENSPECIMEN
IMENSPECIMENSPECIMENSPECIMENSPEC
SPECIMENSPECIMENSPECIMENSPECIMEN
IMENSPECIMENSPECIMENSPECIMENSPEC
SPECIMENSPECIMENSPECIMENSPECIMEN
IMENSPECIMENSPECIMENSPECIMENSPEC
SPECIMENSPECIMENSPECIMENSPECIMEN
IMENSPECIMENSPECIMENSPECIMENSPEC
SPECIMENSPECIMENSPECIMENSPECIMEN
IMENSPECIMENSPECIMENSPECIMENSPEC
SPECIMENSPECIMENSPECIMENSPECIMEN
IMENSPECIMENSPECIMENSPECIMENSPEC
SPECIMENSPECIMENSPECIMENSPECIMEN
IMENSPECIMENSPECIMENSPECIMENSPEC
SPECIMENSPECIMENSPECIMENSPECIMEN
IMENSPECIMENSPECIMENSPECIMENSPEC
SPECIMENSPECIMENSPECIMENSPECIMEN

SALESALESALESALESALESALESALESA
LESALESALESALESALESALESALESALE
SALESALESALESALESALESALESALESA
LESALESALESALESALESALESALESALE
SALESALESALESALESALESALESALESA
LESALESALESALESALESALESALESALE
SALESALESALESALESALESALESALESA
LESALESALESALESALESALESALESALE
SALESALESALESALESALESALESALESA
LESALESALESALESALESALESALESALE
SALESALESALESALESALESALESALESA
LESALESALESALESALESALESALESALE
SALESALESALESALESALESALESALESA
LESALESALESALESALESALESALESALE
SALESALESALESALESALESALESALESA
LESALESALESALESALESALESALESALE
SALESALESALESALESALESALESALESA
LESALESALESALESALESALESALESALE
SALESALESALESALESALESALESALESA
LESALESALESALESALESALESALESALE
SALESALESALESALESALESALESALESA
LESALESALESALESALESALESALESALE
SALESALESALESALESALESALESALESA
LESALESALESALESALESALESALESALE
SALESALESALESALESALESALESALESA
LESALESALESALESALESALESALESALE
SALESALESALESALESALESALESALESA
LESALESALESALESALESALESALESALE
SALESALESALESALESALESALESALESA

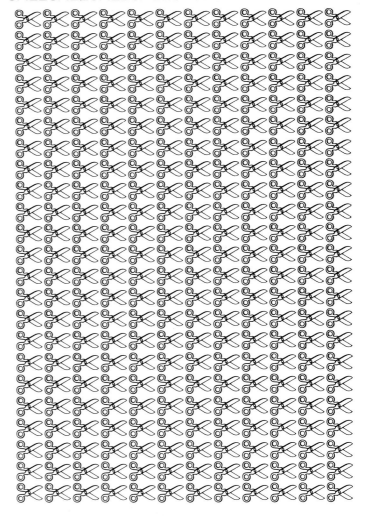

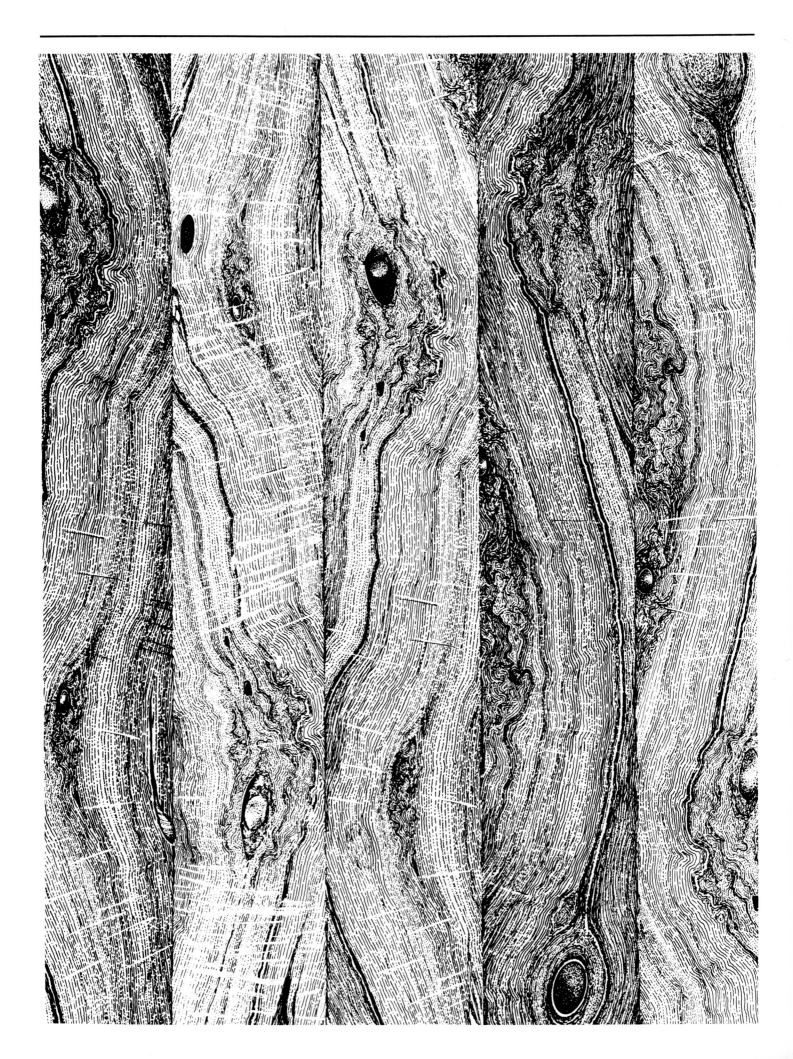